I0836668

Great Aussie Jokes

The Five Mile Press

The Five Mile Press Pty Ltd
950 Stud Road, Rowville
Victoria 3178 Australia
Email: publishing@fivemile.com.au
www.fivemile.com.au

First published 2000
Reprinted 2001, 2002, 2005, 2007
Copyright © The Five Mile Press Pty Ltd
All rights reserved

Editor: Sonya Plowman
Illustrations and cover design: Geoff Hocking
Internal design: SBR Productions
Printed in China

The Little Book of
GREAT
Aussie
Jokes

Edited by Sonya Plowman

The Five Mile Press

Introduction

In the beginning there was nothing, then God said, 'Let there be light.' And there was light. There was still nothing, but you could see it a lot better.

Whether your style of humour is offbeat, good 'n clean or wickedly smutty, you'll find jokes in here that will joggle your funny bone. Of course, you might get yourself into trouble if you tell a blonde joke to the boss's fair wife, or a get-out-of-the-gutter joke to someone's mother. On the other hand, you have different fingers. No, seriously.

Sonya Plowman

Why it's Great to be Woman

1. Free drinks.
2. Free dinners.
3. You can hug your friend without wondering if she thinks you're gay.
4. You know The Truth about whether size matters.
5. You're allowed to be afraid of spiders and other creepy crawlies.
6. Nothing crucial can be cut off with one clean sweep.
7. It's possible to live your life without taking a group shower.
8. Speeding ticket? Why officer, what's that?
9. You can sleep your way to the top.

10. You've never had to walk around school with a jumper strategically placed in front of your crotch.

An old man and an old lady are getting ready for bed one night when all of a sudden the woman bursts out of the bathroom, flings open her robe and yells, 'Super Pussy!' The old man says, 'I'll have the soup.'

The doctor placed his stethoscope on the young woman's chest. 'Big breaths, my dear.' The girl smiled. 'Yeth and I'm only thixteen.'

Bigamist: A heavy fog in Italy.

10 Reasons Why Chocolate is Better than Sex

1. Chocolate doesn't require any pick-up lines.

2. Chocolate satisfies even when it has gone soft.

3. You can eat chocolate in front of your parents.

4. Chocolate doesn't wear socks to bed.

5. The word 'commitment' doesn't scare off chocolate.

6. You can have chocolate in the office without upsetting your colleagues.

7. You can share chocolate with several others without being considered a floozie.

8. A big piece of chocolate is of course better, but even a small piece satisfies.

9. Two people of the same sex can have chocolate without being called nasty names.

10. You can bite into chocolate as hard as you like without causing injury.

One day Jesus comes across an angry, stone-clenching mob encircling a screaming woman. 'What's going on?' he demands.

'She's an adulteress,' cries a voice. 'She must be stoned to death.'

'Let he who is without sin cast the first stone,' replies Jesus, staring back at the crowd. At this, they fall silent, then one by one they drop their stones and shuffle off, ashamed. Except for one little old woman. She staggers up to the adulteress with a huge rock in her arms. She raises it above her head and smashes it down on the other woman, killing her instantly. Jesus lets out a huge sigh and says, 'You know, Mum, sometimes you really piss me off.'

8 Things that Guys Would Love to Say to Women

1. Don't cut your hair. Ever.
2. Sometimes we're not thinking about you. Live with it.
3. Anything we said six months ago is inadmissible in an argument.
4. If you think you're fat, you probably are. Don't ask us.
5. If something can be interpreted two ways, and one of the ways gets us into trouble, we meant the other one.
6. Sunday = sport.
7. No, we really don't want to go shopping with you...
8. Or hold your handbag while you go to the toilet.

What's a catch-22 situation for a Jew?
Free pork!

The mother superior was addressing the
graduation ceremony. 'In the outside world
you will be confronted by many
temptations. You must remember what
you've been taught here. You must cling to

your ideals. You must resist all temptation. For example, a man might try to take sexual liberties with you. Remember that one hour of pleasure could ruin your whole life. Any questions?'

'Yes, Mother. How can you make it last an hour?'

A quiz show on telly had a contestant from Queensland who was asked to complete the following sentence. 'Old Macdonald had a ...'

The Queenslander yelled, 'Farm!'

The compere said, 'Great, well done. Now spell that.'

The Queenslander said, 'E-i-e-i-o.'

A theism is a non-prophet organisation.

An Aussie, a Scot and an Irishman were at a magical fun fair and decided to try the slide. The attendant said, 'Whatever you say on the way down you'll land in at the bottom.' The Scot went first. As he began to slide down he yelled out, 'Money!' and lo and behold, he landed in a pile of bank notes. Then it was the Aussie's turn. He slid down and shouted, 'Money!' He, too, landed in a pile of bank notes. The Irishman was up next. He sat on his little mat and launched himself down the terrifying slide. 'SHIT!' he screamed.

The Irishman went to the brothel and, seeing a BYO sign on the door, went home to get his wife.

The Japanese tourist gave a traveller's cheque to the bank teller in Brisbane. When he counted his money he said, 'Why do I get less money today?'
'Fluctuations,' said the teller.
'And fluck you lot too,' said the tourist.

-and you too!

Two old ladies are sitting in a park, when a flasher walks up, yanks open his raincoat and exposes himself to them. His penis is just hanging right out there, all big, ugly and hairy. This is an enormous shock to the ladies and one of them has a stroke right away! But the other one can't quite reach.

WOW!

A blonde woman went out to check the letterbox. Nothing there. A minute later she went out again to check it; still nothing. Another minute passed by, and she grumpily went to check the letterbox again. Still nothing. 'Is there something wrong?' asked her boyfriend, looking up from the television. 'Sure is. My stupid computer keeps giving me a message saying "YOU'VE GOT MAIL".'

A chicken and an egg are lying in bed. The chicken is smoking a cigarette with a satisfied smile on its beak and the egg is frowning and looking a bit pissed off. The egg mutters to itself, 'Well, I guess we answered *that* question.'

Dating Definitions

Dating: The process of spending lots of money and time in order to sleep with someone.

One night stand: What you call a date where you sleep with someone you really like, but they don't like you enough to bother ringing again.

A friend: A person who is flawed in such a way as to rule them out for dating purposes.

Law of relativity: How attractive a given person appears to be is directly proportionate to how drunk you are.

It was show and tell time, and the kids were describing what they did over the summer holidays. Ben said, 'I rode on a choo.' The teacher said, 'That sounds like fun, but the grown-up word for "choo" is train.' Sally told the class she had visited her nana. 'The grown-up word for "nana" is grandma,' said the teacher. Keith then got up and said, 'I read a book!' The teacher said, 'That's great! What did you read?' The little boy looked very proud and puffed out his chest and said, 'Winnie the Shit.'

How can you tell an extroverted engineer? *When he talks to you, he looks at your shoes instead of his own.*

Computer Terms for the Country Folks

Download: Get the firewood off the ute.

Floppy disk: Result of too much firewood lifting.

Log on: Fire up the barbie.

Log off: Let the barbie cool down.

Monitor: To keep an eye on the barbie.

Laptop: Where the cat sleeps.

Screen: What you shut in the mozzie season.

Modem: What you did to the hay fields.

Website: Under the verandah.

Network: What you do to fix a torn fishing net.

Netscape: When fish escape from the net, as a result of not doing network.

Two nuns are cycling down a cobblestone street. The first one says to the other, 'I haven't come this way before.' The second one says, 'I know, it's the cobbles.'

A man rang home in the early afternoon one day to speak to his wife. The maid answered the phone and told him that his wife was upstairs in the bedroom with her boyfriend. After ranting and raving for a minute, the man asked the maid if she'd like to make a quick $10,000.

'Sure,' she said enthusiastically. 'What do I have to do?'

'Take the gun from my desk and shoot both of them,' he said. The maid went upstairs and did as she had been instructed. She came back down the stairs, picked up the phone, and said, 'Now what do I do with the bodies?' The man replied, 'Take them out the back and throw them in the pool.'

'What pool?' asked the maid. After a moment of silence, the man said, 'Is this 9321 4674?'

An elephant, a penguin, and an Irishman walk into a pub. 'What's going on?' asks the bartender suspiciously. 'Is this supposed to be a joke?'

'I'm telling you mate, that Murray cod I caught last week was six foot long.'

'Well, where is it then?'

'Oh, it broke the line and got away.'

'Well, I fished that same stretch of river a few days ago and was casting near where that old paddlesteamer sank. And I hooked an old lantern. And when I pulled it up, it was still burning.'

'Fair go. You don't expect a bloke to believe that.'

'Well, chop three feet off your Murray cod and I'll blow out the candle.'

Always be frank with your boss. That way, when you screw up, Frank will get the blame.

It's Saturday night and a couple are trying to enjoy the movie but there's a bloke sitting just in front of them moaning and groaning. 'You obviously need medical help. Where are you from?' they said to him.

'The balcony.'

One hundred cardinals were lined up at the pearly gates for admission to heaven. 'Now before I let you in,' said St Peter, 'tell me, how many of you have committed sins of the flesh?' There was silence, and then 99 cardinals raised their hands. Only one didn't. 'Right,' said St Peter, 'off to hell, the 99 of you. And take that deaf bastard with you.'

Classes for Men

1. How to Find the Vacuum
2. You – the Weaker Sex
3. Techniques for Calling Home
4. Beard Shavings are not a Decorative Feature of the Bathroom
5. Farting Techniques Need not be Discussed over Dinner
6. Sexy Underwear is not Comfortable
7. Romanticism – Ideas Other than Sex
8. How to Lose that Beer Gut
9. PMT – Sympathy Goes a Long Way
10. Footy Does not Make for a Fun Weekend

One day while scuba diving Carey was 15 feet below sea level when he saw a guy at the same depth, but without scuba gear. Carey dropped further down, and what do you know, the guy dropped too. Carey was really puzzled by this, and sunk lower, and, true to form, the guy without the scuba gear sunk lower too. Carey couldn't believe it. He took out his waterproof blackboard and wrote, 'How on earth do you manage to stay under water without any scuba gear?' The guy took the board and wrote, 'I'm drowning, you idiot!'

Classes for Women

1. Gossip Sessions – Stop Being a Bitch
2. Elementary Map Reading
3. Gaining Two Kilos Versus the End of the World: A Study in Contrast
4. Driving 101 – Checking the Oil
5. Driving 102 – Flat Tyres do not Equal Nuclear Physics
6. Water Retention – Fact or Fat
7. The Undiscovered Side of Banking – Deposits
8. Shopping 101 – Using Your Own Credit Card
9. Telephone Skills – How to Hang Up

10. Gift-giving Fundamentals
   (formerly Ties Bad – Pin-up Girl
   Calendar Good)

Some drovers were bragging about how smart their dogs were. 'This mongrel of mine,' said one bloke, 'is brilliant. He doesn't just understand simple orders like "sit" and "fetch" – he can follow five-word commands!'
'Tell us another one,' his mates said, jeering and scoffing. So the bloke picked up his dog, threw it in the fire and yelled, 'Bluey, get out of that fire!'

Why did the engineer cross the road? *Because he looked in the file, and that's what he did last year.*

A couple of Indian blokes were in Sydney looking for work at the local employment agency.

'I ran a market stall in Delhi, selling ladies pantihose,' said the first Indian.

'And I was a diesel fitter,' said the second Indian.

'A diesel fitter?' said the employment officer. 'Brilliant. What company were you with?'

'Oh, no company, I worked with my mate on his stall in the market.'

'I don't understand. He sold pantihose. What could a diesel fitter do there?'

'Well, he'd run around the stall yelling out, "Pantihose! Pantihose!" And I'd yell, "Diesel fit her! Diesel fit her!"'

The council's road-building gang had a major problem. They'd gone to work and forgotten to take their shovels. They phoned the foreman to ask advice. 'No need to panic,' he said. 'I'll send the van out with the shovels. But you'll have to lean on each other until they get there.'

A bus of tourists arrived in Kakadu. Everyone got off, except for one old bloke.
'Hey mate, come and see the Aboriginal carving.'
'No thanks,' he said. 'I've lived on a farm all my life and I've seen plenty of cows calving. So I don't suppose it'd be much different.'

Laws of Movieland

1. The car will never start when a bad guy is chasing you.

2. Even the most graceful, athletic women always fall down when being chased by a monster or bad guy.

3. A detective can solve a case much faster when he has been suspended from duty.

4. It's easy for anyone to land a plane providing there is someone to talk it down.

5. The FBI gives their officers personality tests to make sure they are deliberately assigned to a partner who is their exact opposite.

6. All bombs are fitted with electronic timing devices with a big red LCD display so you know exactly when they are going to go off.

7. If a woman hears a strange noise in the middle of the night, she has to go downstairs in her skimpiest lingerie to see what's there instead of leaving the house immediately in her daggy pyjamas.

8. When they are alone, all foreigners speak perfect English to each other.

How many Microsoft executives does it take to screw in a light bulb?
None. They just redefine 'darkness' as an industry standard.

A father-to-be was waiting anxiously outside the labour ward where his wife was delivering a baby. A nurse popped her head around the door and said, 'You have a girl. But there's another on the way, so come back soon.'

'Twins,' he thought, a little shakily. He went away and came back an hour later to be told the second baby had been born, but there was still another on the way. 'Good grief,' he thought. He went to the pub down the street, and after a beer he phoned in and was told a fourth baby was on its way. He started to drown his sorrows. A few stiff whiskies later he called the hospital again, but was so drunk he dialled a wrong number – and got the recorded cricket score. Crying in agony, he collapsed on the floor, a poor, devastated, shuddering and weeping mess. As the barman struggled to pick him up he heard the voice from the phone say, 'The score is 88 all out. And the last one was a duck.'

Doh!

A blonde bought a book at the local bookstore called *Flight to France*. She got back home and was told it was volume four of the encyclopaedia.

FLIGHT -TO- FRANCE

The first day back at school the children
had to report on what they did during
their holidays.

'We went to the Blue Mountains to do
some bushwalking,' said Emily.

'We went camping in Kakadu,' said
Brodie.

'We had a great time,' said Jason.

'We put sticks of dynamite up cane toads'
arses...'

The teacher said, 'Jason! The correct
term is rectum.'

'That's right, miss. Wrecked 'em! Blew
their brains out!'

What's the definition of confusion?
Father's Day in the Western Suburbs.

Did you hear the one about the blonde who was on a spending spree in a shopping centre during a blackout?
She was trapped on the escalator for four hours!

HELP!!

10 Things a Woman Will Never Say

1. I'm bored. Let's have a threesome!
2. Great fart! Do another one!
3. You're so sexy with that beer gut.
4. Let's look at a girlie magazine.
5. Don't worry about forgetting our anniversary. It's okay.
6. Look at her breasts!
7. Shouldn't you be down at the pub with your mates?
8. I've decided to stop wearing clothes around the house.
9. Let's watch footy all weekend.
10. Let's tape ourselves in bed so you can show the guys at work!

How many actresses does it take to change a light bulb?
Just one. They don't like sharing the spotlight.

10 Things Not to Say During Sex

1. What is that?
2. But everybody looks funny naked!
3. You woke me up for that?
4. On second thought, let's turn off the light.
5. Perhaps you're just out of practice.
6. I thought you had the keys to the handcuffs!
7. What did you say your name was?
8. I'll tell you what I'm fantasising about if you tell me what you're fantasising about.
9. When would you like to meet my parents?
10. Was what good for me?

Email is Like a Penis Because...

1. Those who have it would be devastated if it were ever cut off.

2. Many of those who don't have it would like to try having it (email envy).

3. If you're not careful, it can spread viruses.

4. When the system is down, no one is happy.

5. Everybody thinks it's far more important than it actually is.

6. If an email comes with a virus, it can wreak havoc with the whole system and make you wary of using it ever again.

Two men and a woman were sitting in a bar talking about their professions. The first man says, 'I'm a YUPPIE...you know, Young, Urban, Professional.' The second guy says, 'I'm a DINK...you know, Double Income, No Kids.' He then turned around to the woman and said, 'What are you?' She replied, 'I'm a WIFE...you know, Wash, Iron, F**k, Etc.'

A weary traveller stopped at a hotel in the middle of the night, only to be told there were no rooms available. 'Please, you've got to have something,' he begged. 'Even a spare bed somewhere will do.' The hotel manager thought for a moment, then said, 'Well, we do have one spare bed, but it's in a room with a loud

snorer. You probably won't get any sleep.'
'I don't care – I'll take it,' said the
traveller with relief. The next morning
he went down to breakfast bright-eyed
and refreshed. 'So the snorer didn't
keep you up then?' asked the hotel
manager, surprised.
'Nope. As we were going to bed, I bent
over him, kissed him and said,
"Goodnight gorgeous" and he stayed
awake all night to keep his eye on me!'

I think the reason they call them
'Relaxed Fit' jeans is that 'Arse the Size
of Ayers Rock' jeans would not sell very
well.

On the other hand, you have different fingers.

'Madeleine,' said the science teacher, 'please name the organ of the body, which, under the right conditions, expands to six times its normal size.'

Madeleine blushed. 'That's hardly a question to ask a respectable girl.'

'I know the answer!' volunteered Sally. 'It's the pupil of the eye, when it's dark.'

'Correct,' said the teacher. 'And now Madeleine, I have just three things to say to you. Number one, you haven't done your homework. Number two, you've got a filthy mind. And number three, one of these days you're going to be very, very disappointed.'

Despite the cost of living, have you noticed how it remains so popular?

5 Reasons Why God Created Eve

1. God knew that Adam would one day need someone to find the television remote control.

2. God knew that Adam would never remember which night to put the garbage out.

3. God worried that Adam would get lost in the garden because he would not ask for directions.

4. As a method for populating the earth, God knew men would never be able to handle the pain of childbirth.

5. God knew that Adam would never be able to make a haircut appointment for himself.

Two young nuns went to the supermarket in the convent's mini minor. They couldn't find a parking space so one said she'd keep circling the block while the other ducked into the store. Returning with a full trolley, the nun could see no sign of her colleague.

'Have you seen a nun in a red mini?' she asked a policeman.

'Not since I stopped drinking,' he replied.

Telltale Signs of Advanced Parenthood

1. You manage not to laugh when your five-year-old daughter asks for a willy like her brother.
2. You prefer G-rated to R-rated films.

3. You buy matching clothes for you and your six-year-old son.

YEAH?

4. You're no longer embarrassed to be caught singing nursery rhymes on the train.

5. You become addicted to vegemite soldiers.

Two men of the cloth were eating their lunch one day. After the normal small talk about the weather, one said to the other, 'So, I assume you're a catholic priest?' 'That's right. And I guess you're a rabbi?' 'Yes, that's true.' The two munched on their sandwiches for a minute. After a while the rabbi leaned over and whispered, 'Have you ever broken a commandment?' The priest nodded bashfully. 'I slept with a woman once.' He then said to the rabbi, 'Have you ever eaten pork?' The rabbi looked around to make sure no one else was listening. 'Yes,' he whispered. There was a short silence, which was broken by the priest. With eyes sparkling, he said, 'Sex is much better than pork, isn't it!"

You Know You're in Sydney When...

1. Your co-worker tells you they've eight body piercings, but none of them are visible.

2. You can't remember...is dope illegal?

3. You've been to more than one baby shower where the baby has two mothers and a sperm donor as its parents.

4. A really great parking space can move you to tears.

5. You can't decide which adult class to take: aromatherapy, tantric yoga or conversational Burmese.

6. You paid $500,000 for a dank, decrepit one-room flat and it still takes you two hours to drive to work in the CBD.

The Beer Drinker's Survival Guide

Symptom: Feet warm and wet.
Reason: Insufficient bladder control.
Action: Locate nearest dog, complain about house training.

Symptom: Floor blurred.
Reason: You are looking through bottom of empty glass.
Action: Get someone to buy you another.

Symptom: Room seems very dark.
Reason: Bar has closed.
Action: Confirm home address with bartender.

Symptom: Floor moving.
Reason: You are being carried out.

Action: Find out if you are being taken to another bar.

Symptom: You don't recognise anyone around you or the room you're in.
Reason: You've wandered into the wrong party.
Action: See if they have free beer.

Symptom: Taxi floor suddenly looks very colourful.
Reason: Beer consumption has exceeded personal limitations.
Action: Cover mouth.

How do you drive an engineer completely insane?
Tie him to a chair, stand in front of him, and fold up a road map the wrong way.

Books that Didn't Make it Past the Editor's Desk

1. You Are Different and That's Very Bad

2. The Divorce is Your Fault

3. The Pop-up Book of Human Anatomy

4. Dad's New Boyfriend

5. Amanda Was So Bad Her Mum Stopped Loving Her

6. All Dogs go to Hell

7. Your Nightmares are Real

8. Daddy Went Away Because He Doesn't Love You Anymore

9. Poisonous Things that Taste Yummy

10. You Were an Accident

How many movie directors does it take to change a light bulb? *Just one, and when it's finished, everyone thinks that his first light bulb was much better.*

DIRECTOR

Computers are Different in the Movies Because...

1. Computer operators never make typos at crucial moments.

2. Complex calculations and loading of huge amounts of data takes less than three seconds.

3. All computers, in every lab and office, are connected. You can access the information on the villain's desktop computer, even if it's turned off.

4. People never shut the computer down properly.

5. You can infect a computer with a destructive virus by simply typing UPLOAD VIRUS.

6. All monitors are readable from six feet away. And even in a foreign country, the output will always be in English.

7. Powerful computers beep whenever you press a key. Some computers also slow down the output on the screen so that it doesn't go faster than you can read.

8. A hacker is always able to guess the secret password in less than five tries.

9. Computers never crash during highly important activities.

10. The more hi-tech the equipment, the more buttons it has. What's more, these buttons are always very big and colourful.

The 10 Cat Commandments

1. Thou shalt not breathe sardine cat breath in thy human's face.

2. Fast as thou is, thou cannot run through closed doors.

3. Thou shalt not lie down with thy butt in thy human's face.

4. Thou shalt not plonk down on the newspaper thy human is reading.

5. Thou shalt not jump onto thy sleeping human's bladder at 5 am.

6. Thou shalt not leap from great heights onto thy human's genital region.

7. Thou shalt not sit in front of the television or monitor as though thou is transparent.

8. Thou shalt not trip thy humans even if they are walking too slow.

9. Thou shalt not walk in on a dinner party and commence licking thy butt.

10. Thou shalt show remorse when being scolded.

Mal the accountant arrives at the office and, first thing every morning, unlocks his desk drawer to look at a small piece of paper. He then replaces it and relocks the drawer. He does this, every day, for years. Eventually Mal retires, and the accountant at the next desk unlocks the drawer and reads the tattered piece of paper. It says *the debit column is the one nearest the window*.

The butcher still remembered that fateful day when the young woman had come into the shop announcing that the baby boy in her arms was his. By way of support, he grudgingly agreed to provide the woman with free meat until the child turned 18, and had been counting down the years ever since. Finally, the day before his eighteenth birthday the child came to collect some steaks and the butcher told him, 'Well, mate, you can go and tell your mother that's the last free meat you're getting from me. I just wish I could see the expression on her face.'

'Mister, she told me to tell you she's been getting free milk, bread and groceries for the past 18 years, and she wished she could see the expression on your face.'

How many scriptwriters does it take to change a light bulb?
Why do we have to change it?

'My dad's so fast,' said Cameron, 'he can catch a firecracker after it has been lit.'
Not to be beaten, Josh said, 'My dad's faster than that. He can throw a ball and run after it and catch it before it hits the ground.'
'My dad's faster than your dads,' said Tal. 'He works for the City Council. He knocks off at five and he's always home by two-thirty.'

A blind man was walking down the street when his guide dog stopped and peed on his leg. Reaching into his pocket, he took out a biscuit and gave it to the dog. A passer-by who had seen everything was impressed with the man's kindness.
'That's a nice thing to do after what your

dog just did.'
'Not really,' replied the blind man. 'I just
needed to find out where his mouth is so I
can kick him in the balls.'

KICK!

Big Hawk the Indian was with the park ranger one day when they got lost. The park ranger said to Big Hawk, 'Use your tracking ability to get us out of this mess.' Big Hawk bent down and put his ear to the ground. 'Buffalo come.' The park ranger replied, 'How do you know?' Big Hawk said, 'Ear Sticky.'

The three bears returned home from an early morning walk to find the door of their house wide open. Cautiously they went inside. 'Someone's been eating my porridge,' Mama Bear said. 'And someone's been eating my porridge,' Papa Bear said. Baby Bear rushed in. 'Bugger the porridge. Someone's nicked the video.'

An Irishman walked up to the airport ticketing desk and said, 'I'd like a return ticket.'
'Where to?' asked the ticket officer.
'To here!' said the Irishman.

Toe: a device for finding furniture in the dark.

5 Reasons Why Computers Must be Female

1. No one but their creator understands their internal logic.

2. The message 'There is a General Application Error,' is about as informative as, 'If you don't know why I'm mad at you, I'm certainly not going to tell you.'

You call that a *hard* disk!

3. You continually have to liaise with the supplier, even though you'd really rather not.
4. You feel like kicking them when they ignore commands.
5. Sometimes, try as you might, you can't turn them on, particularly if you already have a floppy in.

A blonde was coming home from work. As she turned into her street she noticed smoke coming out of her house. She started yelling, 'Fire! Fire! My place is on fire, come quick!' Then she called the fire brigade. She said, 'My house is on fire, come quick.' The guy asked her how to get there and she said, 'In your big red truck, of course!'

5 Reasons Why Computers Must be Male

1. They have a lot of data, but they are clueless.

2. Big power surges knock them out for the rest of the night.

3. It is always necessary to have a backup.

4. In order to get their attention, you have to turn them on.

5. Size does matter.

How many mystery writers does it take to change a light bulb?
Two. One to screw it in almost all the way and another to give it a surprise twist at the end.

A man saw an advertisement saying 'Porsche for sale! Brand new, only $100'. He thought it must be a mistake, but he thought, 'Well why not, what have I got to lose?' So he went to have a look at the car. The Porsche was brand new, and yes, it was only $100. 'I'll take it!' he said, 'But why are you selling me this great Porsche for only $100?' The lady replied with a bitter laugh. 'My husband just ran off with his secretary, and he told me, "You can have the house and the furniture, but sell my Porsche and send me the money".'

A man put an ad in the classifieds: Wife Wanted. Next day he received 200 letters in the mail. They all said the same thing: 'You can have mine'.

You Know You're an Engineer if...

1. You've spent three hours trying to repair a $10 radio.

2. The sales people at the local computer store can't answer any of your questions.

3. You can quote scenes from any Monty Python movie.

4. You can type 80 words per minute, but can't read your own writing.

5. When you were a kid, Rubik's Cube was your best friend.

6. You have saved every power cord from all your broken appliances.

7. You have more friends on the internet than in real life.

8. You spend more time surfing than watching television.
9. You spent more on your calculator than you did on your wedding ring.
10. Your wife hasn't the foggiest idea of what you do at work.

Two blokes were down at the pub sharing a few beers when the conversation turned to Freudian slips. 'I made the worst Freudian slip last night,' said the first bloke. 'What was it?' asked the other. 'Well, the wife and I were having dinner and I meant to say "Please pass the salt" but instead, by mistake... it just slipped out of my mouth: "YOU'RE RUINING MY LIFE YOU F***ING BITCH!"'

At the end of a job interview the managing director asked the young candidate, who was fresh out of university, what he wanted as his starting salary. The graduate said, 'Well, I think $120,000 a year would be appropriate, depending on what the package contained.' The managing director said, 'Well, what would you say to nine weeks of annual leave, three paid overseas holidays a year, long service leave after five years, and a new Porsche every two years?' The candidate sat up straight, eyes shining, and said, 'Wow! Are you kidding?' The managing director said, 'Yes, but you started it.'

I just got lost in thought. It was unfamiliar territory.

How many fisherman does it take to change a light bulb?
One. And you should have seen it! It was this big!

Why is the person who invests all your money for you called a broker?

A man and his wife were having some problems at home and were giving each other the silent treatment. The next week the man realised that he would need his wife to wake him at 5 am for an early flight to Sydney. Not wanting to be the first to break the silence, he finally wrote on a piece of paper, 'Please wake me at 5 am'. The next morning the man woke up, only to discover it was 9 am, and that he had missed his flight. Furious, he was about to go and see why his wife hadn't woken him when he noticed a piece of paper by the bed. It said, 'It is 5 am, wake up!'

Father O'Brien was greeting his parishioners one Sunday morning when Mary came running up to him in tears. 'What's bothering you, dear?' he asked. 'My husband's just passed away, Father,' she replied. 'Oh Mary,' said the Father, 'That's terrible. Tell me, did he have any last requests?' 'Why, yes he did, Father,' replied Mary. 'He said, "Please, Mary, put down the gun."'

Why did Moses wander in the desert for 40 years?
Even then men wouldn't ask for directions.

20 of Life's Unanswered Questions

1. If all is not lost, where is it?
2. If swimming is so good for your figure, how do you explain whales?
3. What does the Queen sing during the national anthem? 'God save me?'
4. If love is blind, why is lingerie so popular?
5. What is a 'free gift'? Aren't all gifts free?
6. How come you never hear about gruntled employees?
7. Why is 'abbreviate' such a long word?
8. Why are they called 'apartments' when they are so close together?

9. What would chairs look like if your knees bent the other way?

10. If a 7-11 is open 24 hours a day, every day of the year, why are there locks on the doors?

11. Why do people swimming at the beach suddenly get up and go when it starts to rain?

12. Why do women wear shoes that hurt their feet?

13. Why do people look up when they think?

14. If you tied buttered toast to the back of a cat and dropped it from a great height, what would happen?

15. Why are wrong numbers never busy?

16. If it's the tourist season, why can't we shoot them?

17. Where does the white go when the snow melts?

18. What keeps glue from sticking to the inside of the bottle?

19. If you can plant a tree, why can't you tree a plant?

20. How do they get kangaroos to cross at the yellow road sign?

Did you hear the one about the statistician?
Probably.

Do infants enjoy infancy as much as adults enjoy adultery?

Rules for the Workplace

1. The more crap you can put up with, the more crap you are going to get.

2. You can go anywhere you want if you look serious and carry a clipboard.

3. Everything can be filed under 'miscellaneous.'

4. When you don't know what to do, walk fast and look worried.

5. Work hard only when the boss is looking.

6. When the boss walks past your desk, frown and shuffle paper. It promotes a busy look.

Attending a wedding for the first time, a little girl whispered to her mother, 'Why is the bride dressed in white?'
'Because white is the colour of happiness, and this is the happiest day of her life,' answered her mother, keeping the explanation simple. The child thought about this for a moment, and then asked, 'So why is the groom dressed in black?'

Little Red Riding Hood was skipping merrily home when she saw the Big Bad Wolf crouched down behind a log. 'My, what big eyes you have, Mr Wolf,' said Little Red Riding Hood. But the wolf just jumped up and ran away. Further down the road Little Red Riding Hood saw the wolf crouched awkwardly behind a big log again. 'My, what big ears you have, Mr Wolf,' said Little Red Riding Hood. Once again, the wolf ran away! A short while later Little Red Riding Hood saw the wolf once again crouched behind a log. 'Just piss off will ya?' yelled the wolf before Little Red could open her mouth. 'I'm trying to do a number two!'

How to Impress a Woman

Compliment her; cuddle her; kiss her; comfort her; spend money on her; hold her; stand by her; care for her; listen to her; hug her; wine and dine her; go to the ends of the earth for her.

How to Impress a Man

Show up naked.

You've Spent Too Long in the Corporate World if...

1. You believe you never have any problems in your life, just 'issues' and 'improvement opportunities'.

2. You insist upon conducting market research before deciding whether to have another child or not.

3. You write executive summaries of your love letters.

4. Your Valentine's Day cards have bullet points.

5. You give constructive feedback to your dog.

Ever stop to think, and forget to start again?

A man and woman were having drinks when they got into an argument about who enjoyed sex more. The man said, 'Men definitely enjoy sex more than women. Why else do you think we spend 98 per cent of our time thinking about it?'

'That doesn't prove anything,' countered the woman. 'An analogy: when your ear itches and you put your little finger in and wriggle it around, which feels better, your ear or your finger?'

Two Irish hunters were driving through the country to go bear hunting. They came upon a fork in the road where a sign read 'Bear Left' so they went home.

A young boy was having problems learning maths at school, so his parents decided to send him to a private catholic school, hoping the education there would be better. What do you know, after a semester in the new school the boy was getting straight As in all his subjects, even in maths! Surprised, his mother said, 'You must really love it there to be doing so well!'

'Not really,' said the boy, 'It's just that as soon as I saw that guy nailed to the plus sign, I knew they meant business!'

How many art gallery visitors does it take to change a light bulb?

Two – one to do it and the other to say any four-year-old kid could do it better.

A History Lesson

Santa was getting ready for his annual
holiday, but it seemed the gods were
working against him. The deer had come
down with food poisoning, the missus had
just told him the in-laws were coming for a
visit, and the trainee elves were on a go-
slow strike. Frustrated, Santa trudged into
the living room to pour a long glass of
bourbon. Shit. Someone had pinched all
the grog. Fuming, Santa threw down his
empty glass and watched it explode into
bits all over the floor. Just then the
doorbell rang and the cursing,
grumbling Santa stomped over to
answer it. A little angel was standing on
the doorstep with a great big Christmas
tree, decorated with bright red and yellow

baubles. Santa tried to shut the door in the angel's face, but before he could the angel asked ever so sweetly, 'Santa, where would you like me to put this?'
And that, my friend, is how the little angel came to be on top of the Christmas tree.

A drunk stumbles upon a baptism service one Sunday afternoon down by the river. The Minister turns and sees him and says, 'Mister, are you ready to find Jesus?' The drunk looks around him and says, 'Yes, sir, I am.'
The Minister then dunks the fellow under the water and pulls him right back up. 'Have you found Jesus?' the Minister asks. 'No, I didn't!' says the drunk. The Minister dunks him again, brings him up

and says, 'Now, brother, have you found Jesus?'

'No I did not!' says the drunk again. Rolling his eyes, the Minister holds the man under the water for a long time this time, brings him up and demands, 'For the love of God, have you found Jesus yet?!'

The old drunk wipes his eyes and pleads, 'Are you sure this is where he fell in?'

To every rule there is an exception. Except this rule. Err...

If at first you don't succeed, don't take up skydiving.

New Government Warnings on Alcohol

Warning: alcohol consumption is the leading cause of inexplicable rug burns on the forehead.

Warning: alcohol consumption is the leading cause of pregnancy in the world.

Warning: alcohol consumption may lead you to think people are laughing with you.

Warning: alcohol consumption may cause you to thay shings like thish.

Warning: alcohol consumption is particularly lethal at office Christmas parties. Proceed with caution, and be aware you may need to later change jobs.

A couple were sitting in the living room, watching television, when the phone rang. The husband picked it up, listened for a moment and then screamed, 'Damn it! How should I know? Call the weather bureau!' and hung up. 'What was all that about?' the wife asked. 'Aw, some idiot wanted to know whether the coast was clear,' replied the husband.

If a man is alone in the woods talking to himself, and there are no women around for miles and miles, is he *still* wrong?

Three ducks walk into a pub and go up to the bar. It isn't every day that ducks visited his pub so the barman says to the first duck, 'What's your name?'

'Davey,' says the duck.

'How's your day been?' asked the barman.

'Excellent! Been in and out of puddles all day.'

'Oh, that's nice,' says the barman. He turns to the next duck and says, 'Hi. What's your name?'

'Donny,' the duck answers. 'So how's your day been?' asks the barman.

'Great. Had a ball. Been in and out of puddles all day.' So the barman turns to the last duck and says, 'What's your name?'

'My name is Puddles. And don't bother asking about my f***ing day.'

In a bar one night a man was drinking heavily. He'd drink a vodka, walk out to the balcony, and jump off. Minutes later he'd be back again to repeat the whole process. Another customer in the bar asked the guy how he could keep jumping off the balcony without hurting himself.

'It's easy,' the man replied. 'This new brand of vodka provides bouyancy so that when I get near the ground I slow down and land gently.'

'Wow,' thought the other guy, 'I've got to try this!' So he took a swig of vodka, went out to the balcony and jumped off. But splat. He is dead. The bartender looked over to the other guy and said, 'Superman, you're a real arsehole when you're drunk.'

If at first you do succeed, try not to look too astonished.

A man is driving up a steep, narrow mountain road. A woman is driving down the same road. As they pass each other the woman leans out the window and yells, 'PIG!' The man immediately leans out his window and yells back, 'BITCH!' They each continue on their way, and as the man rounds the next corner, he crashes into a pig standing in the middle of the road.

Sometimes I wake up grumpy; other times I let her sleep.

Drive-through ATM Instructions

Procedure for Males

1. Drive up to ATM.
2. Insert card and enter PIN.
3. Enter amount of cash to withdraw.
4. Retrieve card, cash and receipt.
5. Drive off.

Procedure for Females

1. Drive up to ATM.
2. Reverse back one metre to align window to machine.
3. Stall engine.
4. Enter handbag and remove make-up bag and locate card.

5. Check make-up in rear-view mirror.
6. Attempt to insert card into machine.
7. Open door to allow easier access to machine, due to distance from car to machine.
8. Insert card.
9. Re-enter handbag to find scrunched-up paper with PIN number written on inside.
10. Insert PIN, press cancel and re-enter PIN.
11. Enter amount of cash to withdraw.
12. Check make-up and hair in rear-view mirror.
13. Retrieve cash and receipt.
14. Locate purse and place cash inside.

15. Locate cheque book to file receipt.
16. Check make-up again.
17. Drive forward two metres.
18. Reverse back to cash machine.
19. Retrieve card.
20. Locate card holder in purse and put away card.
21. Recheck make-up and hair.
22. Restart engine and pull off.
23. Drive for three kilometres.
24. Release handbrake.

What did the blonde say when she went to check if her indicators were working? *Yes they are, no they're not, yes they are, no they're not.*

During a recent ecumenical gathering, a secretary rushed in shouting, 'The building is on fire!'

The Methodists gathered in the corner and prayed.

The Catholics blamed it on those who had sinned.

The Jews posted symbols on the door hoping the fire would pass.

The Congregationalists shouted, 'Every man for himself!'

The Baptists cried, 'Where is the water?'

The Christian Scientists concluded there was no fire.

The secretary grabbed the fire extinguisher and put the fire out.

Things You Learn From the Movies

1. Honest, hard-working policemen are always shot the day before going into retirement.

2. Should you need to defuse a bomb, don't worry about which wire to cut. You will always choose the right one.

3. If you are blonde and pretty, it is possible to become a nuclear physicist at the age of 23.

4. It doesn't matter if you are heavily outnumbered in a fight involving karate. Your enemies will patiently wait to attack you one by one.

He who laughs last, thinks slowest.